THE
SOLUTION

THE SOLUTION...TO EVERYTHING
Stanley D. Williams, Editor
Hope Smith, Copy Editor

Compilation Copyright © 2024, Nineveh's Crossing, LLC. This registration extends only to the selection, coordination, and arrangement of the content herein, not to the preexisting content itself.

Bible Quotations: Revised New American Bible, Copyright 2019–2024 USCCB
Non-Biblical Quotations:
- www.JesusCentral.com
- www.learnreligions.com/prophecies-of-Jesus-fulfilled
- www.editor's library
- www.YouTube

ISBN (Paperback) - 979-8-9878323-6-3

Library of Congress Control Number:

Printed in the United States of America

Distributed by
Nineveh's Crossing
www.NinevehsCrossing.com
Novi, Michigan USA

TO
EVERYTHING

Having never written anything,
He is the most quoted.

GE
NE
SIS
EXO
DUS
LEVI
TICUS
NUM
BERS
JO
SHUA
DEUTE
RONOMY
JUDGES
RUTH
1SA
MUEL
2SAMUEL
1 KINGS
2 KINGS
2 CHRO
NICLES
1 CHRONICLES
EZRA
NEHEMIAH
ESTHER
JOB
PSALMS
PRO
VERBS
ECCLE
SIASTES
SONG
OF SOLOMON
JERE
MIAH
ISAIAH
LAMENTATIONS
EZEKIEL
HO
SEA
DANIEL
JOEL
AMOS
OBA
DIAH
JONAH
NAHUM
MICAH
HABAKKUK
ZEPHA
NIAH
HAG
GAI
ZE
CHARIAH
MALACHI
MAT
THEW
MARK
LU
KE
JOHN
ACTS
RO
MANS
1 THES
SALONIANS
2 THESSALO
NIANS
1CORIN
THIANS
2CO
RIN
THIANS
GALA
TIANS
EPHE
SIANS
PHILIP
PIANS
CO
LOS
SIANS
TI
TUS
1TIMO
THY
2TI
MO
THY
PHI
LEMON
HEBREWS
JAMES
1 PETER
2PE
TER
1 JOHN
2 JOHN
3 JOHN
JUDE
REVELATION

The Solution...

> In the beginning was the Word,
> and the Word was with God,
> and the Word was God.
> He was in the beginning with God.
> All things came to be through Him,
> and without Him nothing came to be.
>
> John 1:1–3

...to Everything

JESUS

The Solution…

> But a shoot shall sprout from the stump of Jesse,
> and from his roots a bud shall blossom. The Spirit of
> the LORD shall rest upon Him: a spirit of wisdom and
> of understanding, a spirit of counsel and of strength, a
> spirit of knowledge and of fear of the LORD.
>
> Isaiah 11:1–2

...to Everything

JESUS

The Solution…

> Irrespective and irregardless to whatever Evander Holyfield's skills and talent are in the boxing ring, his heart is right with God, and that's what's first and foremost. I have come this far by faith, trusting in [God's] holy Word, leaning on Him, and He's never failed me yet. How does our success come about? Just look up and ask for Jesus Christ, the matchless Lamb, the Prince of Peace … and you will find the answer.
>
> Don King

...to Everything

JESUS

The Solution...

> But you, Bethlehem-Ephrathah
> least among the clans of Judah,
> From you shall come forth for me
> one who is to be ruler in Israel;
> Whose origin is from of old,
> from ancient times.
> Therefore the LORD will give them up, until the time
> when she who is to give birth has borne,
> Then the rest of his kindred shall return
> to the children of Israel.
> He shall take his place as shepherd
> by the strength of the LORD,
> by the majestic name of the LORD, his God;
> And they shall dwell securely, for now his greatness
> shall reach to the ends of the earth: He shall be peace.

Micah 5:1–4a

...to Everything

JESUS

The Solution...

> Therefore the LORD himself will give you a sign:
> The virgin will conceive and give birth to a son,
> and you will call Him Emmanuel.
>
> Isaiah 7:14

...to Everything

JESUS

The Solution...

He never gets farther than an area perhaps 100 miles wide at the most. He does this for three years. Then He is arrested, tried and convicted. There is no court of appeal, so He is executed at age 33 along with two common thieves. Those in charge of his execution roll dice to see who gets his clothing—the only possessions He has. His family cannot afford a burial place for Him so He is interred in a borrowed tomb. End of story? No, this uneducated, property-less young man has, for 2,000 years, had a greater effect on the world than all the rulers, kings, emperors; all the conquerors, generals and admirals; all the scholars, scientists and philosophers who have ever lived—all of them put together. How do we explain that—unless He really was what He said He was?

Ronald Reagan

...to Everything

JESUS

The Solution...

> The angel answered, "The Holy Spirit will come on you, and the power of the Most High will overshadow you. So the holy one to be born will be called the Son of God."
>
> Luke 1:35

...to Everything

JESUS

The Solution...

                              Do whatever He tells you.

                                        Mary
                                     John 2:5

...to Everything

JESUS

The Solution...

> In the realm of character, Jesus has the field.
> The lips of the world are dumb and silent before
> the question of finding anything better. Men need
> a goal of character and Jesus is that goal.
>
> E. Stanley Jones

...to Everything

JESUS

The Solution...

And the Word became flesh
and made his dwelling among us,
and we saw his glory,
the glory as of the Father's only Son,
full of grace and truth.

John 1:14

...to Everything

JESUS

The Solution...

> The Spirit of the Lord God is upon me, because the
> LORD has anointed me; He has sent me to bring
> good news to the afflicted, to bind up the broken-
> hearted, to proclaim liberty to the captives,
> and release to the prisoners.
>
> Isaiah 61:1

...to Everything

JESUS

The Solution...

> Had the doctrines of Jesus been preached always as pure as they came from his lips, the whole civilized world would now have been Christian.
>
> Thomas Jefferson

...to Everything

JESUS

The Solution...

> You are the Messiah, the Son of the Living God.
>
> Simon
> Matthew 16:16

...to Everything

JESUS

The Solution...

> Follow me.
>
> John 1:43

...to Everything

JESUS

The Solution...

> I say unequivocally that the evidence for the resurrection of Jesus Christ is so overwhelming that it compels acceptance by proof which leaves absolutely no room for doubt.
>
> Sir Lionel Luckhoo

...to Everything

JESUS

The Solution...

We have found the Messiah.

Andrew
John 1:41

...to Everything

JESUS

The Solution...

> You must make your choice. Either this man was,
> and is, the Son of God, or else a madman,
> or something worse.
>
> C. S. Lewis

...to Everything

JESUS

The Solution...

> Come and you will see.
>
> John 1:39

...to Everything

JESUS

The Solution...

I wasn't put on this Earth to play basketball, although I love to play and I love to compete. And it's a great avenue for me to experience special moments when I can help people. Two things are sacred to me—my family and my religion. I am never embarrassed by Jesus Christ. Without Him I wouldn't be in the position I am today.

Karl Malone

...to Everything

JESUS

The Solution...

> Rabbi, you are the Son of God;
> you are the King of Israel.
>
> Nathanael
> John 1:49

...to Everything

JESUS

The Solution...

> I'll just say, "For God so loved the world that He gave his only begotten Son, that whosoever believes in Him, should not perish, but have everlasting life." I am trusting Christ's death for me to take me to heaven.
>
> Mickey Mantle

...to Everything

JESUS

The Solution...

> For the Son of Man has come to seek and to save what was lost.
>
> Luke 19:10

...to Everything

JESUS

The Solution...

Our country needs a savior right now. And, no, it's not me. It's someone much higher. The life, and death, and resurrection of Jesus Christ forever changed the world. The founding of our great country could never have happened without Jesus Christ and his followers and his Church. Jesus Christ is the ultimate source of our strength and freedom.

Donald Trump

...to Everything

JESUS

The Solution...

> Then the eyes of the blind shall see,
> and the ears of the deaf be opened.
> Then the lame shall leap like a stag,
> and the mute tongue sing for joy.
> For waters will burst forth in the wilderness,
> and streams in the Arabah.

Isaiah 35:5–6

...to Everything

JESUS

The Solution...

> They think to order all things wisely; but having rejected Christ they will end by drenching the world with blood.
>
> Fyodor Dostoyevski

...to Everything

JESUS

The Solution...

Come to me, all you who labor and are burdened, and I will give you rest. Take my yoke upon you and learn from me, for I am meek and humble of heart; and you will find rest for yourselves. For my yoke is easy, and my burden light.

Matthew 11:28–30

...to Everything

JESUS

The Solution...

> Whoever wishes to come after me must deny himself, take up his cross, and follow me.
>
> Matthew 16:24

...to Everything

JESUS

The Solution...

> I can't imagine more surprising places for God to appear than a manger or a cross. Yet all through his life and resurrection, Jesus demonstrates the power of showing and sharing God's love.
>
> Fred Rogers

...to Everything

JESUS

The Solution...

> I have told you this so that you might have peace
> in me. In the world you will have trouble,
> but take courage, I have conquered the world.
>
> John the Baptist
> John 16:33

...to Everything

JESUS

The Solution...

> I came under conviction when I was in the third grade, and I talked with my mother. I told her, "I don't understand this, but I need to talk to you." We talked, and she led me to Jesus. The following Sunday I made a public confirmation of my faith. In one sense, it was not terribly eventful for an eight-year-old, but it was the most important event in my life.
>
> John Grisham

...to Everything

JESUS

The Solution...

> He must increase; I must decrease.
>
> John 3:30

...to Everything

JESUS

The Solution...

> Real men do live for Christ. It is important to make your peace with Christ while the opportunity exists. Life is so fragile that you never know when it's going to be over. It could be over in the blink of an eye, and then it's too late to accept God's gift of salvation.
>
> Chuck Norris

...to Everything

JESUS

The Solution...

> Everyone who drinks this water will be thirsty again; but whoever drinks the water I shall give will never thirst; the water I shall give will become in him a spring of water welling up to eternal life.
>
> John 4:13–14

...to Everything

JESUS

The Solution...

> A thief comes only to steal and slaughter and destroy; I came so that they might have life and have it more abundantly.
>
> John 10:10

...to Everything

JESUS

The Solution...

> When you look at the reasons why Christ came, why He was crucified—He died for all mankind, He suffered for all mankind. So that, really, anybody that transgresses needs to look at their own part or their own culpability. It's time to get back to a basic message, the message that was given....
> He forgave as He was tortured and killed.
>
> Mel Gibson

...to Everything

JESUS

The Solution...

> I am the way and the truth and the life. No one comes to the Father except through me.
>
> John 14:6

...to Everything

JESUS

The Solution...

> I think that everybody that loves Christ or knows Christ, whether they are conscious of it or not, they are members of the Body of Christ.... That is what God is doing today. He is calling people out of the world for His name, whether they come from the Muslim world, the Buddhist world, the Christian world or the non-believing world. They are members of the body of Christ because they have been called by God.
>
> Billy Graham

...to Everything

JESUS

The Solution...

> I am the vine, you are the branches. Whoever remains in me and I in him will bear much fruit, because without me you can do nothing.
>
> John 15:5

...to Everything

JESUS

The Solution...

> My kingdom does not belong to this world.
> If my kingdom did belong to this world,
> my attendants [would] be fighting
> to keep me from being handed over to the Jews.
> But as it is, my kingdom is not here.
>
> John 18:36

...to Everything

JESUS

The Solution...

> They open their mouths against me,
> lions that rend and roar.
> Like water my life drains away;
> all my bones are disjointed.
> My heart has become like wax,
> it melts away within me.
> As dry as a potsherd is my throat;
> my tongue cleaves to my palate;
> you lay me in the dust of death.
> Dogs surround me;
> a pack of evildoers closes in on me.
> They have pierced my hands and my feet;
> I can count all my bones.
> They stare at me and gloat;
> they divide my garments among them;
> for my clothing they cast lots.
>
> Psalm 22:14–19

...to Everything

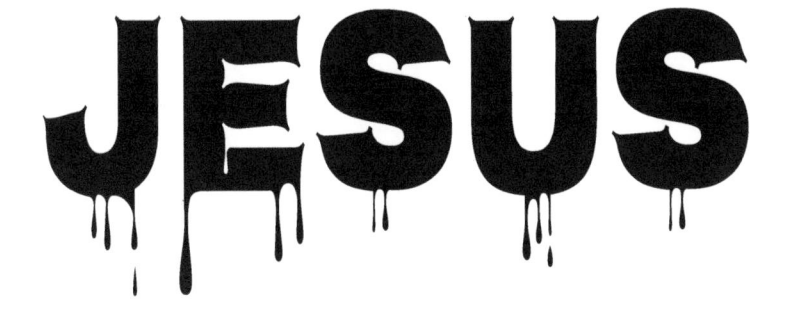

JESUS

The Solution...

> He was spurned and avoided by men,
> a man of suffering, knowing pain,
> Like one from whom you turn your face,
> spurned, and we held Him in no esteem.
> Yet it was our pain that He bore,
> our sufferings He endured.
> We thought of Him as stricken,
> struck down by God and afflicted.
>
> Isaiah 53:3–4

...to Everything

JESUS

The Solution…

I pray and meditate every single day, every morning. You know, I pray in cabs. I pray in airplanes. I don't really ask for anything—I just pray that Jesus will give me the strength to follow Him. That's all I pray for. And that I will always turn my will and my life over to His care.

Lawrence Kudlow

...to Everything

JESUS

The Solution…

> But He was pierced for our sins,
> crushed for our iniquity.
> He bore the punishment that makes us whole,
> by his wounds we were healed.
> We had all gone astray like sheep,
> all following our own way;
> But the LORD laid upon Him
> the guilt of us all.
>
> Isaiah 53:5–6

...to Everything

JESUS

The Solution...

Christ, who being rich became poor and emptied Himself to work out our redemption, calls us: to share in His poverty so that we might become rich through His poverty; to bear witness to the true face of Jesus—poor, humble, and friend of sinners, the weak and the despised.

Mother Theresa

...to Everything

JESUS

The Solution...

> Though harshly treated, He submitted
> and did not open his mouth;
> Like a lamb led to slaughter
> or a sheep silent before shearers,
> He did not open his mouth.
> Seized and condemned, He was taken away.
> Who would have thought any more of his destiny?
> For He was cut off from the land of the living,
> struck for the sins of his people.

Isaiah 53:7–8

...to Everything

JESUS

The Solution...

It is a very good thing that you read the Bible....
The Bible is Christ, for the Old Testament leads
up to this culminating point ... Christ alone ...
has affirmed as a principal certainty, eternal life,
the infinity of time, the nothingness of death,
the necessity and the *raison d'être* of serenity and
devotion. He lived serenely, as a greater artist than
all other artists, despising marble and clay as well
as color, working in living flesh. That is to say,
this matchless artist ... made neither statues nor
pictures nor books; He loudly proclaimed that He
made ... living men, immortals.

Vincent van Gogh

...to Everything

JESUS

The Solution...

> He was given a grave among the wicked,
> a burial place with evildoers,
> Though He had done no wrong,
> nor was deceit found in his mouth.
> But it was the LORD's will to crush Him with pain.
> By making his life as a reparation offering,
> He shall see his offspring, shall lengthen his days,
> and the LORD's will shall be accomplished through Him.

> Isaiah 53:9–10

...to Everything

JESUS

The Solution...

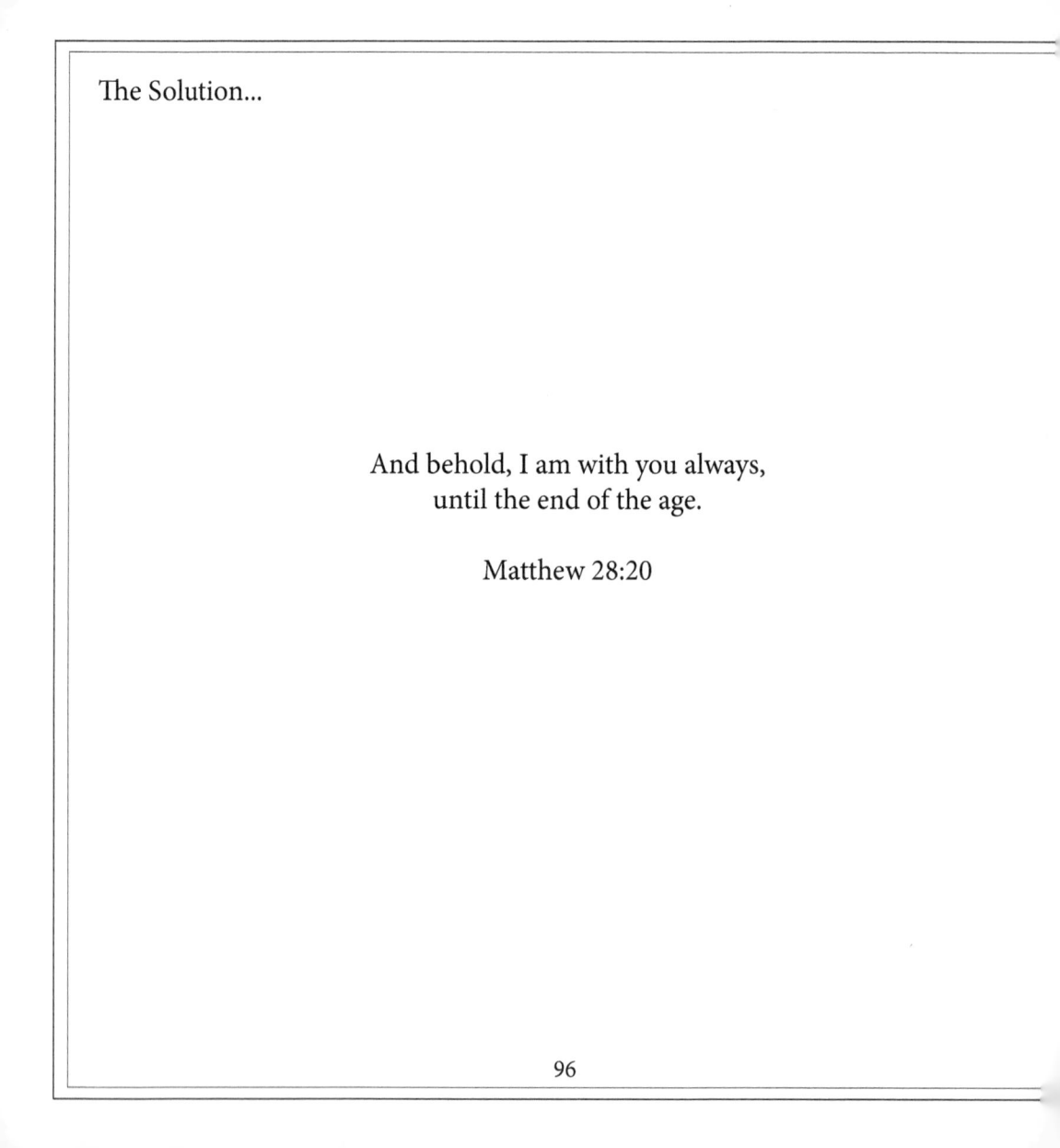

> And behold, I am with you always,
> until the end of the age.
>
> Matthew 28:20

...to Everything

JESUS

The Solution...

> Do not be afraid. I am the first and the last,
> the one who lives. Once I was dead, but now I am
> alive forever and ever. I hold the keys to death and
> the netherworld.
>
> Revelation 1:17–18

...to Everything

JESUS

The Solution...

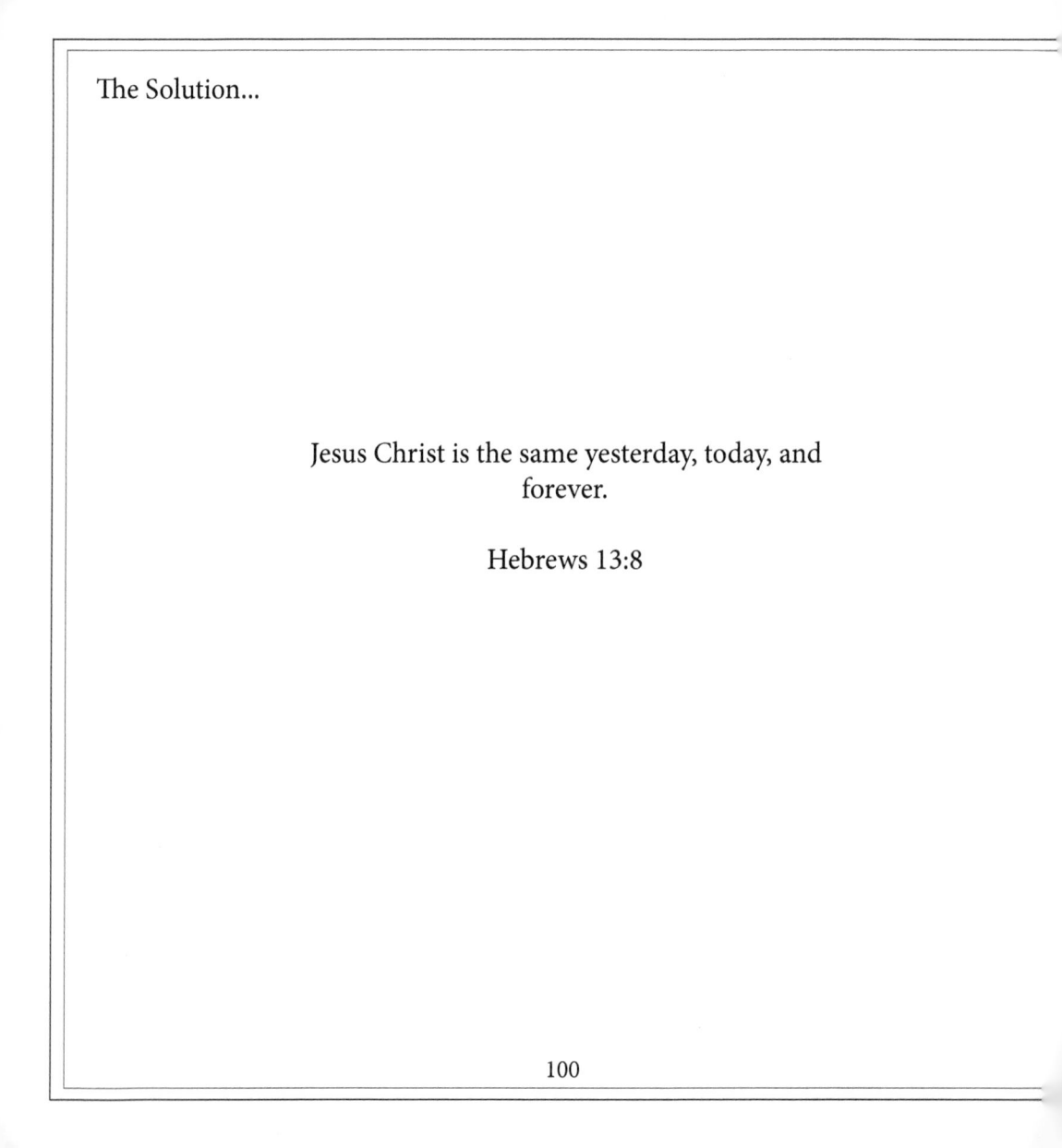

> Jesus Christ is the same yesterday, today, and forever.
>
> Hebrews 13:8

...to Everything

JESUS

JESUS Adobe InDesign Font Index

Layout: Adobe InDesign Mac
Basic Text - Minion Pro 12
3 Britanic Bold **JESUS**
5 Academy Engraved LET   JESUS
7 American Typewriter   JESUS
9 Jazz LET   **JESUS**
11 Adlery Pro   *JESUS*
13 Apple Chancery   *JESUS*
15 Alumni Sans Inline One   **JESUS**
17 Bank Gothic   JESUS
19 Baloo   **JESUS**
21 Baskerville   JESUS
23 Chalkduster   JESUS
25 Monotype Corsiva   *JESUS*
27 Cracked   **JESUS**
29 Didot   JESUS
31 Emblema One   **JESUS**
33 Desdemona   JESUS
35 Edwardian Script ITC   *JESUS*
37 Curlz MT   JESUS
39 ITC Tiffany Std   **JESUS**
41 Giddyup   *JESUS*
43 Kegger   **JESUS**
45 Copperplate Gothic Light   JESUS
47 Luckiest Guy   **JESUS**
49 Pauline   *JESUS*

51 Oleo Script Swash Caps   *JESUS*
53 Synchro LET   JESUS
55 Rosewood Std   **JESUS**
57 Filmotype Jade   *JESUS*
59 Hiragino Kaku Gothic StdN   **JESUS**
61 Onyx   JESUS
63 Lobster   *JESUS*
65 Harrington   JESUS
67 Bauhaus 93   **JESUS**
69 Imprint MT Shadow   JESUS
71 Kino MT   **JESUS**
73 Herculanum   JESUS
75 Black Ops One   **JESUS**
77 Matura MT Script Capitals   *JESUS*
79 Lucida Blackletter   *JESUS*
81 Nosifer   **JESUS**
83 Colonna MT   JESUS
85 Marker Felt   **JESUS**
87 Braggadocio   **JESUS**
89 Santa Fe LET   *JESUS*
91 Microsoft Yi Baiti   JESUS
93 Mystery Quest   **JESUS**
95 Mona Lisa Solid ITC TT   JESUS
97 Sisters   **JESUS**
99 Zaphino   *JESUS*
101 PortagoITC TT   **JESUS**